The Grateful Road
What I Have Learned

Chris H. Norman

Richmond, Virginia

THE GRATEFUL ROAD
What I Have Learned
Copyright © 2008 by Chris H. Norman

All photographic content from iStockphoto and dreamstime in accordance with royalty and rights provisions set forth in each.

Family photograph by Carolyn Evans.

Clementine Charles Publishing
ISBN: 978-0-6151-9984-9

Cover design by Charlie and Clemie Norman
Second Printing
Printed in the United States of America.

<u>Overview</u>

A gift to his two children, the author describes what he has learned in his life. It is a reminder that all time is borrowed, and that there is much to be grateful for in this beautiful world as we grow on this journey called life.

<u>Praise for *The Grateful Road*</u>

"This is a beautiful, beautiful book. Chris Norman writes from a place that meditating monks and ascetics aspire to but few arrive at...the essence of pure being. We are all born into this state, but seem to lose it along the way.

   As we read Chris's words, his perceptions and images awaken that state of pure being to us. We 'see' the world around us with fresh eyes, teeming with life, love, meaning, and goodness, all shining and new. What a gift!"

—JOHN MAXWELL TAYLOR, Author of *The Power of I AM: Creating a New World of Enlightened Personal Interaction*

" '*The Grateful Road*' comes straight from the heart of one who knows the joy of life. In direct and simple, yet eloquent language, Chris Norman shares the way he found how to live by active love. I feel richer for having read his infallible guidelines."

—WALTER STARKE, Author of *It's All God, and Joel Goldsmith and I: The Inside Story of a Relationship with a Modern Mystic*

"Spiritual energy soars in this book! With simplicity, sincerity and great love, Chris Norman has captured the essence of what he calls the 'forever lessons' of life and Life. These are the lessons that all of us are here to learn and to live. Chris's thoughts are a profound and deeply meaningful gift—not only to his children Charlie and Clemie, but also to everyone who reads this exquisitely written treasure."

—MICHAEL C. RANN and ELIZABETH RANN ARROTT,
Authors of *Shortcut to a Miracle: How to Change Your Consciousness and Transform Your Life*

"Chris Norman's book is a sweet reflection of life that will touch anyone's heart that is open to receive such a life treasure."
—JOAN GATTUSO, Author of *A Course in Love, A Course in Life,*
and to be released in autumn of 2008, *The Lotus Still Blooms.*

" *'The Grateful Road'* is a wake up call to fully appreciate the life we have been given and all of the chapters that we pass through on the journey."
—CAROLINE SUTHERLAND, Author of *The Body Knows*

" *'The Grateful Road'* is a poignant reminder that whether our days are long or short, it is the connection between us and our awareness of the beauty of the moment that we experience day after day, that is life. Chris reminds us that the culmination of our life defines our return to the Source of Life; we are measured less by our material successes and more by our relationship with G-d and one another. A must read for those seeking a deeper meaning of our day to day life experience."

—RABBI SUZANNE H. CARTER, *President of the International Federation of Rabbis.*

To Renee, with eternal love and gratitude.

ALWAYS

As I move from here into eternity
I will be one with the wind that blows through the trees.
I will be one with the birds that soar with such ease.
I will be one with the waves loose in the sea.
I will be one with the planets and expanding galaxies.

I will also be one with God's love that engulfs you and me.
I will also be one with your fears and any anxiety.
I will also be one with your laughter, and all the good times to be.
I will also be one with your accomplishments in this life journey.

We will always, always be one,

you and me.

Contents

<u>*Acknowledgements*</u>

To Chris Daniele, whose magic pen can make the written word, in whatever form, sparkle and be meaningful. Also to Brenda Robinson, whose loving support made this possible. To the many who have contributed to this small manuscript, including: Nancy Norman, Senior Minister of Unity of Delray Beach, Florida; Cathy Norman, Minister of Unity of Ventura, California; and Gene Norman. It is beyond words to describe what their love and support mean to me.

By no means is that it. I am forever indebted to the leadership of the most dynamic and innovative organization I have had the privilege of being associated with: Mike Schliesmann, John Davis, and Bill Raaths of the great, Great Northern Corporation. 'Thank you' is just not enough.

Introduction

Sooner or later all of us come to a place in our development where we begin to question. Without the knowledge of a greater meaning to life, we become restless, lacking a sense of grander purpose. Sometimes it takes a shock to see life anew. The day before my 50th birthday, several leading neurologists gave me a diagnosis that no one wants to hear. I was told that I have Lou Gehrig's disease, also known as Amyotrophic Lateral Sclerosis, or ALS for short. Very little is known about this disease. It is a rare degenerative neurological condition with no treatment. No one can tell you how long you will live with ALS. I might have three months. I might have three years. No one knows.

What I do know is that I have time, whether it is three months or three years. As an individual seeking answers, I am very grateful. Time to reflect is a precious gift. It allows me to take stock of my life: to understand what went well, what didn't go so well, and what I have learned in this life. Memories are the milestones I study. The experiences of my life are what I have to learn from. They are etched and final for all of eternity: the small acts of kindness when no one was looking, the summer nights chasing fireflies, playing hide-and-go-seek, contagious laughter, the taste of great wine and deep philosophical discussions, and finally, the self-centered hurtful things I did or said to my fellow human beings. They are unchangeable; ready for review like a familiar book.

As I turn the pages of this book, common themes emerge. I have learned that life is much more than being born, growing up and maturing; it is a rhythmic experience of mistakes and successes adding to knowledge, dreams and expression. Our journeys take us from suffering to joy, ultimately leading us to larger parts of ourselves.

We are all in this journey together, evolving and growing in our connection to each other and with God, however defined. As my eyes open, I learn that we are kind, loving creatures, working our way back home, and yes we make mistakes along the way. That is part of the process. We are all developing into something new, leading to other beautiful beginnings and the realization that life, wherever we find ourselves in this great universe, is awesome and majestic.

Lou Gehrig called ALS "the bad break". It is. I am soon to leave family and friends that I love beyond any possible ability to put into words. Each night, however, when everyone is asleep, the phones have stopped ringing and the world has slowed down, I sit and marvel at the enormity of it all and how the universe and its trillion moving pieces all seem to work. I am in awe of the interconnectedness of life, from a blade of grass to the movement of the galaxies. I am in awe of our role in this majestic drama and how privileged we are to be here. I am in awe of the unconditional love our Creator cradles us with and how it bonds us all.

Reviewing my life, I see there were other opportunities to laugh, to play, make more mistakes, and, yes, to love more. Like most of us, I dedicated myself to activity until activity consumed me and then I forgot what it was I set out to do in the first place, moving me further into the maya, or the illusion, that separates us all. The reality is that life is constantly teaching us, if we just choose to stop from time to time to accept the lessons. I have discovered that kindness and love are the most important things we can share. I am humbled by the effect kindness has had on me and others in my life. Kindness connects us. It elevates, inspires, liberates, and transforms us. In the words of Mother Teresa, "Acts of kindness echo on forever." It is in this vein that the following pages are written. It is unadorned, shared in the hope that what I have learned in this life will serve my two children in their lives, as well as you and yours.

There is much to be grateful for on this road called life.

Letter to Charlie and Clemie

Dear Charlie and Clemie,

Don't ever let anyone tell you there is no such thing as magic. In front of you lies the miracle of love, the adventure of accomplishment, the enchantment of friendship, and ultimately, the blessing of being able to learn life's lessons in a universe where every tree, every flower, every blade of grass is magnificently unique. There is magic everywhere.

What lies before you is a journey towards joy and love. It is a beautiful process. In keeping with the natural ebb and flow of the universe, progress usually does not happen in a nice straight line: there will be challenges and setbacks. We move forward and then we move back, then we move forward again.

Throughout this journey it is not what happens to you that defines you, it is how you react. Please remember that hate, anger, and resentment are poisons. These are enemies to joy. They make you and the world you live in smaller. It takes strength to be kind, to forgive, and to love. The reality is that we are on this planet to grow and help others grow. As we create lives filled with abundance and love, we provide loving links, renewing, rejuvenating, and wonderfully inspiring whoever we come into contact with.

Life is the "immense" journey. We only have one life to experience it. Every day, hour, minute, and second is yours to do with what you want. It is a gift from God. It is your heritage. Much like a garden, tend your life wisely. Plant and nurture seeds that are good, and manage the weeds – they happen. Make sure your garden is your very own. Each flower in the field, each blade of grass, each sunrise and sunset, each snowflake is absolutely unique. Nature abhors sameness. There has never been a better you, and there never, ever will be.

My personal journey has been great. It has brought me through the trials of adolescence into adulthood, coming into contact with sparkling souls whose love are now part of me. I am larger because of this. It has brought me into contact with people from remote third world villages to the upper levels of social society. It has made me appreciate good manners and kindness. It has given me a vocation that has been one of my greatest joys. I have rarely worked a day in my career and I still go to bed dreaming about what I do for a living. For this I am unbelievably grateful.

Through time you will connect with the majesty of an individual relationship with God. Never let third parties interfere with this. It is your personal relationship and it is the most important thing you can do. As you grow in spiritual warmth of this unfathomable love, your mission in life will begin to take on a greater purpose: you will become *intentional* beings, armed with the command of forgiveness, the beauty of kindness, the power of intention, and the majesty of unconditional love. It is then that you will realize that we are all connected to each other. It is then that you will understand that what we learn here are forever lessons, as we are forever beings.

I want you to know that I am so proud of you and who you are becoming. You are both brave of heart and inquisitive of mind. Hold on to your sense of humor and your ability to play. It will keep you young throughout your life. Be bold in what you want. You have amazing potential. Desiring, aspiring, and yearning are natural and will help you achieve in this world. We know that by focusing intentions and efforts we attract people and circumstances to what we want to accomplish. As Emerson stated: "Once you have made a decision, the universe conspires to make it happen." We live in a world that is abundant, bountiful, and awesome in its enormity, reflecting an endless kaleidoscope of life treasures to experience.

Know that throughout your experience, the universe supports you, whether you are aware of it or not. When you work, work with your entire being, with the enthusiasm that you were born with. When you rest, let Him hold you.

I love you forever,

Dad

Jan. 2008

Richmond, Virginia

The Grateful Road
What I Have Learned

Chapter One

Playing and laughing are the healthiest things we can do

"In every real man a child is hidden that wants to play."
Friedrich Nietzsche

Children have it right. Their world is a place of wonderment and excitement. I recently watched a game of duck, duck, goose, in my neighborhood. It restored and rekindled me. Listening to their laughter I knew that we live in a universe where playing and laughter are integral, otherwise God would not have given us these incredible gifts.

A healthy human is one who can play, find the humor in simple things, smile quickly and laugh deeply. Life somehow feels brighter and lighter as we reconnect to what is good.

Several years ago, we had family Thanksgiving in a large three story house we were renovating. What started off as the children playing hide-and-go-seek within innumerable nooks and crannies throughout the residence, turned into a game that included the whole family, over thirty of us. Even Aunt Julia, who was approaching seventy, participated. The game lasted late into the night. We experienced each other as we never had before. That night we forgot about Uncle John's terminal cancer. That night we didn't worry about the national debt or the fact that we were living in the middle of a national crack epidemic. We laughed. We played. We connected.

During the evening, one of our friends hid so well we simply couldn't find him. We looked throughout the house and even went outside searching for him. We contemplated calling the police. I wonder how we would have explained that one: "Well you see officer, we were playing hide-and- go- seek and we lost him". In any event, there was a sewing room on the top floor and our friend had rolled himself up in a bolt of fabric and leaned himself against the wall with the other bolts of fabric. The only way we found him was when we noticed a tuft of his hair sticking out of the top of fabric bolts!

Our friend died of cancer several years later. He said that night was one of the best times he had ever had. He was 35 years old.

Life forces us away from play as we "grow up". Doubting whether our lives have meaning we work that much harder, moving further away from the joys of simple play and laughter. The late Leo Buscaglia put it splendidly: "In a world that knows no shortage of nonsense, we shouldn't hesitate to happily and playfully add our own touch of insanity. It is one of the best ways to survive." It is also one of the best ways to immunize you from day-to-day frustration.

As a young man, I experienced what laughter can do to transcend age, language and culture. We called ourselves the "four amigos". Together we traveled the South Pacific island of Fiji. One day, as daring young men, we took an open-sided bus to what we thought was an exotic beach, only to find, after many hours on an exhausting bumpy dirt road, we were moving deep into the muggy jungle. The driver, with a toothless smile, politely dropped us off at a solitary building, and in halting English, informed us a returning bus would be there later that night or possibly the next morning. The "four amigos" were left stranded to wait on an old wooden porch of a lonely country store. We had our hearts set on a glamorous beach where beautiful, single European women lingering with fruity drinks in their hands. We waited and waited until, being curious and wanting to stretch, I walked down a path behind the store and was surprised to find a small native village with a dirt plaza in the middle. Several children in the corner of the square were playing soccer and kicked the ball to me, starting a championship game of Fijian soccer (Rules of Fijian soccer: a game with no rules). The laughter and the dust we kicked up drew attention. Smiling faces emerged: children, toddlers, parents, and elders came out to watch, most of them barefoot. We played and laughed without thought of past or future. The eternal present was ours until we could move no more.

Using clumsy hand signs I indicated there were others back at the road. With that, this large group of smiling faces strolled to the store, surprising my amigos. None of the villagers knew English and we most certainly did not know Fijian. We looked at each other awkwardly, trying to communicate until someone brought a guitar onto the porch. "Row, Row, Row Your Boat" was a favorite. We sang that night, we danced that night, and we laughed that night and shook that old, wooden porch. When a bus did arrive later in the evening, we were reluctant to leave. I still remember looking back as we jostled down that jungle road; a solitary light bulb from the country store shone down on some of the loveliest people I have ever had the privilege to know.

They were waving goodbye and smiling.

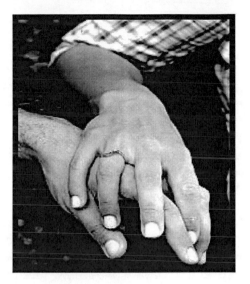

Chapter Two

Kindness can transform lives

"At times our own light goes out and is rekindled by a spark from another person."

Albert Schweitzer

Every act of kindness, like a pebble thrown into a still pond, creates ripples. Acts of kindness magnify. They strengthen and unite. However small, they are some of the most important things we can do. The check out clerk, the parking attendant, the restaurant server and the homeless all have emotions, feelings, dreams and inner identities shielded from life's challenges. A simple smile, an encouraging word, a helpful hand can lift and absolutely transform, regardless of circumstance, age or culture. The great Chinese philosopher Lao Tzu wrote that "Kindness in words creates confidence, kindness in thinking creates profoundness, and kindness in giving creates love."

My sister Cathy used to visit me when I lived in Venezuela. One day we went to a street-side cafeteria close to where I worked. There was a little shoeshine boy who was either homeless or came from a very poor family. He stood at the restaurant entrance hoping someone would buy him a meal. My sister and I, seeing the child, invited him in. After eating what we thought was a very full plate, the boy went back in line for seconds, then thirds. I can still see his peaceful smile, sleeping on the table bench. From that point on, I made sure he had lunch whenever I was there. He would always go back for seconds, thirds and then fall asleep smiling like an angel, in absolute contentment, without a care in the world. This was one of the first memories that came to me after being diagnosed with ALS. Driving back from the hospital that day I wondered where that boy is now and I wish I had done more for him than just buy him lunch. "I pass through this world but once" William Penn wrote several hundred years ago. "Any good thing therefore that I can do, or any kindness that I can show to any human being, let me do it now. Let me not defer it or neglect it, for I shall not pass this way again."

The real story of your life and mine is not about where we go, or what we have, but how we grow along the way. Our souls are not defined or trapped by a name, a position in society, our net worth; we are defined by the people we help along the way. As Ann Landers put it, "The true measure of a man is how he treats someone who can do him absolutely no good." The reality is that there are an amazing number of selfless and very kind people in this world. The people that sustain the Salvation Army, Hospice, Habitat for Humanity, the Muscular Dystrophy Association, the ALS Association, The Red Cross and the many Children's Hospitals are angels on earth. At no time in our history are more people working for others unselfishly, either through organizations or in one-on-one efforts. Our best hope lies in acts of kindness without the expectation of reward.

As George Elliston put it: "How beautiful a day can be when kindness touches it!" Cecil B. DeMille added to this when he wrote, "As I look back upon my life, I find that the things in which I take the deepest and most lasting satisfaction are the things that involved giving more than getting."

Kindness is love in action. A dear colleague of mine always gives money to beggars. He has no moral dilemma in this as he believes that regardless of how they got to their situation they are brothers and sisters. Several months ago, caught in slow moving traffic going into New York City at the end of the George Washington Bridge, he had a life-affirming encounter. Teetering in median there was an elderly gentleman holding a hand written cardboard sign that read "Hungry". My friend approached, rolled down the window and gave him money. The beggar showed intense gratitude and as he flashed a beautiful smile, he was transformed from an old and withered drifter to a youthful presence beaming unconditional love, stunning my friend. Behind a car horn honked, breaking the spell and instinctively my colleague drove forward losing sight of the panhandler. If the man teetering in the highway median was a mere mortal down on his luck or a celestial angel, it doesn't really matter. This is the stuff of kindness.

Chapter Three

Forgiveness is a gift you give yourself

"Forgiveness is almost a selfish act because of its immense benefits to the one who forgives."

Lawana Blackwell

I have learned that individuals who have cultivated forgiveness in their lives have a sense of power and peace. It provides energy empowering enthusiasm and wellbeing. When we realize resentment is a product of our own reactions, it is a day to celebrate, as we begin to reclaim our power and control our lives. We start to heal. This is why Jesus told his followers "Love your enemies, bless them that curse you, and pray for them which despitefully use you" (Matthew 5:44). The Dalai Lama put it this way: "The truly courageous is able to withstand harm without the corrosive suffering that hatred and anger bring." He went on to say, "Tolerance and patience do not imply submission or giving into injustice."

Forgiving is one of the most difficult things we do in life, but it is impossible to fully live when we cannot let go. The author Alan Cohen said that holding resentment and ideas of unforgiveness are like drinking a glass of poison and expecting the other person to die. When we harbor resentment toward another person we are bound to them and we can never completely heal. Yesterday is gone. Ill feelings and negative emotions serve no purpose other than to denigrate our spiritual and physical health. No matter what happened, it is over; we cannot go back. The present is the thing that we have. Any hardship, real or imagined, can be undone and transformed. "Hatred stirs up trouble; love overlooks the wrongs that others do." Proverbs 10:12.

Liberating myself from the burden of resentment is a priority for me. At the top of my list of people for whom forgiveness work was needed was a senior executive who I never got along with. In truth, our relationship was quite hostile. Struggling with how to go about forgiving, I prayed and asked God to help, thinking it unlikely I would ever see or talk to this individual again. Soon enough, when I was at the airport, stranded in a wheelchair waiting for my flight by the gate, I noticed him out of the corner of my eye in a large crowd moving through the terminal. I shouted, but it was too late. He disappeared down the corridor. Desperately, I yelled in hope that he would hear me. "What a shame," I thought. What a wasted opportunity to directly forgive and release. Having turned my attention back to my work, I looked up one more time and saw him glancing at me around the corner.

Walking straight to me he said: "I understand that you have some health issues."

"Yes I do, but we are going to make this as positive as possible." I went on, "Let me ask you a very important question. Are you and I all right?"

He bent over and hugged me. "You and I are fine." The long standing loathing and resentment dissolved into unconditional love, causing an upwelling of pure emotions in both of us. I felt unbelievably liberated, as I believe he did too, because he stumbled back into the crowd.

While it may seem we become vulnerable when we forgive, in truth we become stronger. The more we forgive, the more we understand forgiveness, the stronger we become. Mozes Kor and her twin sister, Miriam, suffered cruel genetic experiments for nearly a year at the hands of Dr. Josef Mengele, the ruthless "god of Auschwitz", an experience that would haunt them all their lives. During a search to find medical files in hope of shining light on her persistent and debilitating condition, Mozes met a former SS medical officer, a Dr. Munch, whom many testified had helped or saved their lives. Meeting the doctor was a revelation. He too had nightmares.

"I immediately realized that I had the power to forgive. That no one could give me the power and no one could take it away. And for a little victim, who was a victim for almost 50 years, to realize that I have the power, made me feel very good."

Kor invited the doctor to join her at Auschwitz on the 50th anniversary of liberation. During the anniversary visit, Munch signed his paper documenting the gas chambers and Mozes Kor read and signed her declaration of forgiveness. "I felt immediately a burden of pain was lifted from my shoulders. That I was no longer a prisoner of my tragic past. That I was no longer a victim. That I was finally free," she said. This experience lead Kor to embrace self-healing through forgiveness, going so far as to forgiving Mengele and the Nazis for the atrocities they inflicted upon her and her family. Kor maintains forgiveness is empowering, liberating and the only way to end the cycle of violence and hate.

Mozes now tells everybody, "Forgive your worst enemy. It will heal your soul. It will set you free."

Chapter Four

We learn from our problems

"You are today where your thoughts have brought you. You will be tomorrow where your thoughts take you."

James Allen

The first of the "Four Noble Truths" Buddha taught was "Life is suffering." Life presents problems. The question becomes: Do we master or do we moan? When the world challenges us, we tend to invest power in things that were never meant to have influence over us: the remote control, food, alcohol or drugs. The Greek root for the word problem, *proballo*, means to "throw in front of." Problems, regardless of size, do not go away. They are obstructions, barriers that require attention. I have learned that you can't drink them away, you can't complain them away, you can't run away from them. By confronting and resolving problems, life begins to have meaning and we grow into larger parts of ourselves. In the words of Benjamin Franklin, "Those things that hurt, instruct."

Problems challenge us to expand. It is in the valleys where we grow the most. It is in the valleys where we reconnect with the deep and lost parts of ourselves and bring forth courage, faith, and inspiration. No truer words are found than with Oliver Goldsmith, the 17th century Irish poet: "Our greatest glory is not in ever failing, but in rising every time we fail." This is the stuff of life. Thoreau said, "If one advances confidently in the direction of his dreams, and endeavors to live the life he has imagined, he will meet with success unexpected in common hours."

People who achieve do not have fewer problems than people who fail. It is just that achievers, regardless of endeavor, understand that ours is a cause and effect world. This is recognized by science (for every action, there is a reaction) and religion ("As you sow, so shall you reap"). "If we want more roses," novelist George Eliot observed, "we must plant more!"

Successful people are much like farmers. Farmers plant seeds with conviction. Their intention is pure. The farmer does not worry about what crop will show up in his field, he knows. He planted corn and he will harvest corn. The power of intention touched by faith opens the channels through which blessings flow abundantly and freely. A friend who succeeds in everything he does says it this way: "In a way, I live my life backwards. I visualize what I want and work my way towards it with every fiber of my being. I know that what I intend and nurture will grow and manifest into my life." Great people create their lives actively, as opposed to those who wait passively to see where life takes them next.

Study unusually successful people and you will find them imbued with an enthusiasm for their work that is contagious. Not only are they excited about what they are doing, but they get you excited. Enthusiasm is one of the greatest assets in the world. As Emerson said, "Nothing great was ever achieved without enthusiasm." Psychologist and social scientist Albert Mehrabia's oft-cited study showed the words we use account for only seven percent of the impact of communication. The other 93% is the result of voice quality and appearance – or how we say what we say. Enthusiasm is a major part of this. Enthusiasm is an invincible power that overcomes problems, small and large just as put forward in Ezekiel in the Old Testament: "And in every work that he did, he did with all his heart and prospered."

Goethe explained that "the greatest thing in the world is not so much where we stand as in what direction we are moving." Many achievers manage to see big goals for themselves and work tirelessly towards them through intention, communion with God, and inspired action. Spurred by motivation, they do not let petty things get them stuck. Resentments and obstacles are dealt with immediately to ensure a flow of prosperity throughout their world. Wherever you find yourself, enthusiastically plant positive seeds of intention, and, as Ralph Waldo Emerson once wrote:

"Hitch your wagon to a star!"

Chapter Five

Emotions only have the strength we allow

"Remember, no one can make you feel inferior without your consent."
Eleanor Roosevelt

In Lewis Carroll's *Alice in Wonderland,* Alice recoils in terror before the Queen of Hearts, who proclaims "Off with her head!" Alice is about to succumb to panic when she realizes, "Why, you're nothing but a pack of cards!" They then all fly away. There is plenty to scare us in life. We are constantly reminded of egregiously hurt victims, turmoil in the Middle East, an epidemic of drugs and alcoholism, the rising divorce rate, and the fact that the economic recession is coming and it will probably be very bad this time. Worry is a prayer about what you do not want in your life. Focusing on troubles, real or imagined, draw them forward with gathered strength. As Job said, "That which I feared hath come upon me."

Problems are caused by beliefs that limit, that take hold in our consciousness. The most damaging are related to fear, doubt, jealousy, anger, envy, regret, low self esteem, and their insidious mutations. The great commentator Ernest Holmes referred to these as "enemies of wholeness." What I have learned is that thoughts and emotions only have the strength we allow. As we become aware of our own patterns of thought and how they impact our lives, we notice emotionally immature individuals who are enslaved by anger, impatience and criticism. These are people who see what is wrong in life. Regardless of circumstance, they find fault. P.D Ouspensky observed: "The strangest and most fantastic fact about negative emotions is that people actually worship them."

The reality is, we own our thoughts and feelings. No one, no thing, no circumstance, can make us feel anything. We are free souls with our lives to do with what we want. It is a gift from our creator – it is our heritage. We decide how to invest this time and power. It is a simple decision; how we want to live?

ALS is a disease that robs you of life "one tablespoon a day," as Philip Simmons, a fellow sufferer put in his book, *Learning to Fall, The Blessings of an Imperfect Life.* Each morning I wake up and forget about my condition until I try to move. It is then that I take stock of "what is left" and reconnect with the good in life, remembering that "I am the master of my fate, the captain of my soul" as the British poet William Ernest Henley wrote in his epic poem, *Invictus*, over 150 years ago. The title, *Invictus*, is Latin for "unconquered." At the age of twelve, Henley became a victim of tuberculosis of the bone. In spite of constant physical and medical challenges, Henley persevered and survived to lead an active life for nearly 30 years. The poem was written from a hospital bed.

Out of the night that covers me,

Black as the Pit from pole to pole,

I thank whatever gods may be

For my unconquerable soul.

In the fell clutch of circumstance

I have not winced nor cried aloud.

Under the bludgeoning of chance

My head is bloody, but unbowed.

Beyond the place of wrath and tears
Looms but the Horror of the shade,
And yet the menace of the years
Finds, and shall find me, unafraid.

It matters not how strait the gate,
How charged with punishment the scroll,
I am the master of my fate;
I am the captain of my soul.

We were born to shine like stars across the sky. As expressions of God, we are always greater than any problem, experience, or situation.

It is simply a matter of choice.

Chapter Six

Praying feels good

"By prayer man renders himself capable of receiving."

Thomas Aquinas

I have learned that life is so much easier with prayer. Connecting with the loving presence Jesus talked about just plain feels good. It is nice to have a partner on this journey called life. I cherish what Father Rhabanus of the German Jakobsberg monastery said: "Entrusting our lives to a higher power does not make us needy, rather it opens our eyes and makes us truly free. Accepting that we do not need to do everything ourselves." He goes on to say "Trust God with your disappointments, even your complaints. You will find it liberating. It will comfort you and give you a place to rest." Mother Teresa's thought builds on this: "Feel often during the day the need for prayer and pray. Prayer opens the heart, till it is capable of containing God himself. Ask and seek, and your heart will be big enough to receive Him and keep Him as your own."

Anything can be a prayer. Singing can be a prayer. Dancing can be a prayer. Anything: whistling, writing, painting, however we choose to connect with God. Theologian Peter Kreft said in this regard: "Prayer is the great conversation." It is a yearning of the heart. Worrying about "the right way" to pray just gets in the way. It is an obstacle to the beautiful relationship waiting for us through prayer. Benedictine author and teacher, Joan Chittister, writes "The important thing to remember in the spiritual life is that religion is a means, not an end." She goes on to say "When we stop at the level of the rules and the laws, the doctrines and the dogmas—good guides as these may be—and call those things the spiritual life, we have stopped far short of the meaning of life, the call of the divine, the fullness of the self."

Prayer empowers. It provides strength and energy. As one individual put it, "Prayer is the most powerful form of energy one can generate. It is a force as real as terrestrial gravity...When we pray, we link ourselves to the inexhaustible motive power that spins the universe." The Bible continuously tells us of the power of our prayers. In Isaiah 55:11 it says, "My word shall not return to me void, but shall accomplish that whereunto it is sent." Also, "Whatever things you desire, pray and believe you shall have them." Mark 11:24.

We hear of miraculous stories of prayer. My story occurred when I was twelve years old living in Caracas, Venezuela. There were five of us who thought it would "be really neat" to explore one of the many sewage tunnels under the city. We found two torches at the tunnel entrance and bravely walked forward to explore world's unknown. Excitedly, we worked our way though tunnel mazes until we could hear people talking in the high rises above us. Turn after turn, deeper and deeper under the city we went. We probed further and further until we stumbled into a large rat nest. Our torches fell into the water and absolute blackness engulfed us somewhere under the city of Caracas, without any knowledge on how to get back. The screams were deafening.

We held each other while the seriousness of the situation started to hit home. No one knew we were exploring sewage tunnels. Feeling the sides of the tunnel we attempted to make our way back. As we proceeded the tunnel became smaller. Terror increased with each step through rats, cockroaches, and deepening sewage water. We eventually felt some fresh air and noticed light. What we thought was an exit was a highway grate with cars zooming across it. There was no way we could escape and not get hit. It was then that we lowered our heads and prayed. I can still feel the intensity of that prayer; five little boys reaching out to God with every part in their being. We went back into the darkness, determined to survive. There was this "knowing" we would get out. No more tears or crying. Our fears ended with the prayer. We knew we would be saved. To this day I do not remember how we got out. What I do know is that the sun was setting when we emerged from the sewage system, miles from where we entered.

Outside, the five of us dropped to our knees.

Chapter Seven

It is impossible to be grateful and not be happy

"Gratitude is not only the greatest of all virtues, but the parent of all others."

Cicero (106 BC -43 BC)

Each year my son Charlie and I would hike up Crab Tree Falls in Virginia, the second tallest waterfall on the east coast. We have tried to make it an annual rite of passage that started when he was nine years old. The trail is in an isolated section of the Shenandoah Valley. Usually there are a handful of hikers making their way up the trail along side the waterfall, but there have been times when we are the only ones making the climb. At top of the mountain is an unobstructed view of nature that is everything Virginia is known for. In the fall, when leaves change color, from bright yellow to crimson to deep purple, one is surrounded by a prismatic blaze of color. Long winged birds glide the drafts below, the sun shines, and the water moves rapidly down the valley. Time stops. It is then that everything is

all right with the world. You cannot help but to be thankful.
What I have learned in life is that:

It is impossible to be bitter when one is grateful.

It is impossible to be unhappy when one is grateful.

It is impossible to be without hope when one is grateful.

I have learned that being thankful energizes the good around us. When you find truly successful individuals, you will find gratitude in large quantities. The question becomes: How do we become grateful? The human mind is an amazing thing in that whatever it is looking for, it tends to find. If you are looking for injustice, you'll have no problem finding it. If you are looking for happiness, you will find it. It is the same with gratitude. Genuine happiness happens when we make a personal commitment to see life as a gift. It is a personal decision. We then become aware of the multitude of blessings everywhere.

*If you woke up this morning with more health
than illness, you are more blessed than the
million who will not survive the week.*

*If you have food in your refrigerator, clothes on
your back, and a roof over your head and a
place to sleep, you are richer than 75 percent of
the world.*

*If you have money in the bank or in your wallet,
you are among the top 80 percent of the world's
wealthy.*

*If you hold up your head with a smile on your
face and are truly thankful, you are blessed
because the majority can, but most do not.*

Author Unknown

As one very dear friend put it, "We connect with God when we are thankful." In so doing we rise above SELF when we are thankful. In human circles this means we rise above self-serving, self-condemnation, self-importance, self-gratification, self-seeking, self-righteousness, self-glorification, self-centeredness, self-consciousness, self-indulgence, self-deception, selfishness.

In other words, we move outside ourselves when we are thankful, and start the journey towards grace.

Chapter Eight

It is never too late

"If I knew the world was going to end tomorrow, I would still plant a tree today."

Otto Frank (Anne Frank's father)

"In spite of everything, life is good."

Anne Frank

If I could meet anyone from any time in history, high on my wish list would be Anne Frank, the little Jewish girl forced into hiding during the Holocaust. She and her family, along with four others, hid for 25 months in a cramped annex of rooms with one window where she could catch a glimpse of ". . .chestnut tree and a patch of blue sky." Ultimately, Anne was arrested and deported to Nazi concentration camps where she died of typhus at the age of fifteen. Her diary describes what it was like growing up as a young girl with eight others in small living quarters during one of the most wretched times in human history. In spite of this, she somehow managed to connect with an uplifting spirit that has inspired generations— "Then I do not think of all the misery, but of the glory that remains." She went on to say "Go outside into the fields, nature and sun, and seek happiness in yourself and in God. Think of the beauty that again and again discharges itself within and without you and be happy." Reading her diary, one gets the sense that she lived as though each moment, each day lived was precious. "In spite of everything, life is good."

I have learned that it is never too late to break the chains of guilt, remorse, self-incrimination and victim hood that hold us back. It is never too late to make amends, to be kind, to love, and connect with the magic, regardless of where we find ourselves. Shakespeare wrote: "Every day is a fresh beginning. Every morn is the world made new." The words of the poet Philip Doddridge have always inspired: "Awake my soul! Stretch every nerve, and press with vigor on; A heavenly race demands thy zeal, and an immortal crown."

Recently, a nurse practitioner came into my room asking if I would receive a visitor. Another person with Lou Gehrig's disease wanted to meet me. "By all means!" I said. "This ALS stuff is lonely; it would be nice to have company." In walked Scott. We shook hands and started comparing notes. His disease was not as advanced as mine, but we both knew that our time on this planet was limited. He stated "I don't blame anyone for this. I don't blame God. I am looking at this as a growth experience and I will use what time I have left to its fullest advantage." I was blown away. My new best friend Scott. With the time left, he and I will be together on our final journey, taking advantage of any day we are blessed with.

Time is unbelievably precious.

Chapter Nine

Friendship is love

"My friends are my estate."

Emily Dickinson

I once accidentally ran a friend of mine over in a golf cart. He forgave me. That is friendship. I ran him over again several months later. He forgave me again. That's love. A friend is another part of ourselves; it is a gift we give ourselves. Friendships sustain us. Friends connect us to life. And yes, friends forgive us.

What is a friend? It is someone who:

- Walks beside you and accepts you as you are.

- Believes in you and doesn't give up on you.

- Values and understands you.

- Raises your spirits.

- Forgives your mistakes.

- Helps and supports you.

- Inspires you to be the best you can be.

- Loves you for who you are.

Life is made rich by the friends made along the way. As Kahlil Gibran put it, "And in the sweetness of friendship let there be laughter, and sharing of pleasures. For in the dew of little things the heart finds its morning and is refreshed."

Bud and my dad met in high school. Dad broke his leg playing football and Bud showed up asking if there was anything he could do. That was over 65 years ago. They have been friends ever since. No road is completely smooth; they weathered differences of opinion and separation of time and geography, but they always seemed to return to each other. Dad tries to see Bud daily in the nursing home. Bud has Alzheimer's and is bedridden. Dad knows that somehow, even on the bad days, Bud smiles inside when he shows up with coffee and his favorite Danish. On these down days, Dad sits next to the bed and talks or reads aloud to Bud. Then there are the good days when Bud is lucid and they reminisce about the "old times." Once, Dad asked him "Bud how come you remember things we did 50 years ago, yet you don't recall me being here yesterday?" Bud replied, "Gene, I have got to prioritize my memories with what I have left." They both laughed, and then Bud reached out and held dad's hand "I do miss you when you are not here." Dad's current day relationship with Bud reminds me of a quote found on a recent Internet blog, "A friend is someone who knows the song in your heart, and can sing it back to you when you have forgotten the words."

What true friends have in common is each other's best interest throughout life's peaks and valleys. It is one of the greatest treasures we are blessed with on this journey of life.

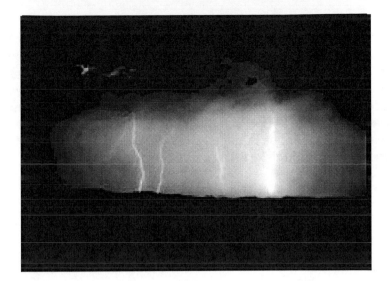

Chapter Ten
Anger destroys

"Nothing can bring you peace but yourself."
Ralph Waldo Emerson

When we look at the barriers to love and happiness we inevitably find self-justified emotions of anger. Anger is both an emotion and a coping mechanism. If one is angry, it is impossible to be happy and loving in dealing with oneself and others. As Ken Keyes wrote in *Handbook to Higher Consciousness*, "A loving person lives in a loving world. A hostile person lives in a hostile world."

I have learned that people who are angry feel devalued, rejected, unloved or powerless in some way. They use anger to shield themselves from further hurt. It is easy to react to negativity with negativity. Many think that anger is power. The trap is this: it is a state of weakness and makes one's world smaller. True courage and power lie in the ability to forgive and love oneself and others, regardless of what has occurred. As we focus on patience and love, we begin to unshackle the chains of anger, remorse and resentment.

We move from the prison of negativity, becoming free souls who refuse to dwell on past injuries. We can then experience hurt and not let negative emotions rule us. We move towards what Jesus taught; an inner peace that passes all understanding. When we embrace this, we recognize that there is no such thing as justifiable anger and that there is no such thing as justifiable resentment. The *Tripitaka*, (the earliest of Buddhist writings) called The Way of the Doctrine, or the Buddhist proverb, put it this way:

> *If a man speaks or acts with an evil thought, pain follows him, as the wheel follows the foot of the ox that draws the cart.*
>
> *If a man speaks or acts with a pure heart, happiness follows him.*
>
> *By thoughtfulness, by restraint and self control, the wise man may make for himself an island which no flood can overcome.*
>
> *Though a man go out to battle a thousand times against a thousand men, if he conquers himself he is the greatest conqueror.*
>
> *Good people shine from afar, like the peaks of the Himalayas.*

Emanuel Swedenborg wrote that we will not be in Heaven until Heaven is in us. This is a path of true peace, and a quality you carry throughout life, regardless of circumstance.

Chapter Eleven

We live in a world of miracles

"There are only two ways to live your life. One is as though nothing is a miracle. The other is as though everything is a miracle. Look deeply, and you will find a miracle today, in your very midst."

Albert Einstein

Some time ago, I was separated from my travel companions as we motorcycled our way through the hills of the ancient and exotic countryside of Indonesia. Each person I asked for directions would attempt to help with sign language, which only added to the confusion. With unmarked roads and a language so foreign, it seemed as I continued I was further and further away from where I needed to be. Riding over a hill, a majestic valley appeared. Dismounting the bike, I stood at the edge of this solitary mountain dirt road and watched the sun's rays pass through the mist below producing a rare double rainbow. Jeweled sparkles played against a canopy of deep green creating a luminous dance. Standing next to me was an elderly woman in a much-worn native dress, balancing a brown package on her head. We were the only ones on the ridge. She briefly turned her head and returned my smile as if to say "I know, I know." Time had slowed and the world seemed to stop as we watched the universe show off below. Philosophers speak of such life-affirming instances, when we merge into some sort of singularity, and even though we have few explanations of how or why, we become lost in the wonder of it all.

Many of us lose awareness of the magic around us. We bombard ourselves with wishes, doubts and fears. Our lives are a tangled web of hopes, dreams, worries, and uncertainties. We subject ourselves to doubt and fear in a bountiful world where life germinates and manifests itself everywhere. We claim there is no such thing as the miraculous, even though we live in a universe where each flower in the field, each blade of grass, each sunrise and sunset, each snowflake, each person is absolutely unique. I believe that if we understood the miracle of a single flower our whole life would change. We would marvel at the enormity of it all and how the universe with all of its trillion moving pieces somehow seems to work. Walt Whitman came to the same realization towards the end of his life "I believe a leaf of grass is no less than the journey-work of the stars."

We live in a miracle. We just need to be aware of it.

Chapter Twelve

Love what you do and what you do will love you back

"A man must get his happiness out of his work."

Thomas Carlyle

I have never met anyone who has achieved substantial success doing something they hated. It just doesn't happen. One of the keys to success is to link passion with avocation. Make your passion your profession and you will never work a day in your life. Personally, I love what I do. I dream about my work. I cherish the people I work with and count them as my dearest friends. We have a sense of common purpose and unity; we are successful. This is one of the great blessings in my life and it epitomizes what Kahlil Gibran wrote in *The Prophet* that "Work is love made visible."

95% of Americans are not satisfied with their work, according to surveys. They do not have fulfillment. Nothing is gained with people suffering in unsatisfying jobs. Living within self-imposed limits does not serve the universe. Rumi, the 13th century poet, put it this way:

> *You were born with potential.*
>
> *You were born with goodness and trust.*
>
> *You were born with ideals and dreams.*
>
> *You were born with wings.*
>
> *You were not meant for crawling, so don't.*
>
> *You have wings.*
>
> *Learn to use them and fly.*

When you have found your calling it can be an expression of love, as Joan D. Chittister, who wrote an article called *How Shall We Live* put it, "Work is our gift to the world. It binds us to the rest of humankind and to the future. It saves us from self-centeredness and leads to fulfillment. It gives back as much as we take from life." If you believe in what you are doing you will experience fulfillment and joy. Everyone around you will believe and become energized as well. The world around you becomes a better place.

In the 21st Century, there are great needs. The world needs people to find their passion, from health care, business, real estate development, the arts, or whatever it might be. It would make it a better place, especially considering the following by Dr. T. Roberts of Tulane University.

"If we could shrink the Earth's population to a village of precisely 100 people, with all existing human relations remaining the same, it would look like this:

- There would be 57 Asians, 21 Europeans, 14 from the Americas and 8 Africans.

- 50% of the entire world's wealth would be in the hands of only 6 people and all 6 would be citizens of the United States.

- 80 would live in substandard housing.

- 70 would be unable to read.

- 50 would suffer from malnutrition

There is a tremendous amount of work to do on this planet.

Chapter Thirteen

Everything is Packaging

"Perception is reality."

I have come to realize that everything is packaging. How we put ourselves together. How we present ourselves. Science is confirming what we knew all along: we live in a world of first impressions. What is startling is the time it takes for the average human being to size up a person, product or situation, is not minutes as we once thought, it is actually done in milliseconds. Malcolm Gladwell presents the latest research in his book, *Blink*, on the fact that we have the capacity to sift huge amounts of information, isolate telling details and come to astonishingly accurate conclusions in seconds.

My first exposure to the power of perception was with a smaller company that made bug zappers. They were trying to hold onto their share of the market. The rest of the market was dominated by one competitor, whose product was not really too different from that of my client. A bug zapper is a bug zapper. The job of a bug zapper is to zap bugs. The only difference was the package. One was dull and boring, the other glossy and smart. We spiced up the packaging (at 3X the cost) and over a three year period their bug zappers took over half the market. We didn't change the product, just the package.

Whenever we interface with the outside world we are being

judged, whether we like it or not. Perceptions and judgments happen swiftly and what I have learned is that you only have one shot to make a first impression. The second thing I have learned is that people can rapidly sense phoniness. Nothing is more disturbing than people who pretend, who are duplicitous rather than straightforward and honest. As long as we come from the heart and we are genuine about who we are, results and perceptions are real. Genuine efforts result in genuine response. When we live in harmony with our core values we can be straight forward, honest, and up-front. This is the way we build trust, the foundation of all relationships, whether it is with a rice farmer in Nepal or in an executive boardroom.

It is also the best way to show the world who you are.

Chapter Fourteen

Happiness is what happens when we give happiness away

"Happiness is like perfume, you can't spray it on others without getting some on yourself."

Anonymous

I remember going for a run one late afternoon on a desolate path in the Connemara region of western Ireland. This is the part of Ireland where villagers give directions by pubs and churches, not street signs- "Well you see, you turn right at Bobby McGee's, then proceed to St. Edwards, and if you see the father don't tell him I'm at Paddy's Pub…" It was the end of a great day and I was clearing my head as I ran through fields to get a view of the Atlantic Ocean. There was a desolate feeling about the place that matched the cool wet day, typical of Ireland. A more austere scene would be hard to imagine. The land stretched before me with an endless succession of hills rolling down to the ocean edge and the carcass of an abandoned castle stood on the hill behind. It no longer had a roof and the floors had long since rotted away.

The thick, tall, grey stone walls looked down the sloping fields to the ocean, as if they were on some sort of eternal watch. In all that space there was one human form far away, tending his sheep. He saw me, turned and started in my direction. His dog bounded full speed, jumped over a rock wall and greeted me like a long lost relative.

He was an elderly man with a face that reminded me of the great Irish actor, Peter O'Toole. Here was a 21st century man complete with an iPod and expensive Nikes with a country sheep herder.

"It's strange to see others here," he stated. "My name is Caler." He was a thin man with wispy brown hair that protruded from a worn woolen cap. He asked if I would like to hear some poetry.

"I love poetry!" I responded. He recited several poems, and one especially moved me. It was a simple poem written by a young girl 160 years ago during the height of the potato famine. He said she lived in the castle behind us. It spoke about how this girl loved her home and how content she was, and the fact that she did not want to leave. What I remember is only the first part:

"I will never be as happy as I am in my tree.

Strong limbs hold me as I look to the sea

I know not, care not, what will become of me

I only know now that I am happy."

I imagined this young girl who climbed trees, who ran through the fields catching butterflies, and who played in the rain. Looking back at the castle remnants, the poem made me wonder whatever became of her. Did she and her family survive the potato famine? Did she know love? What did she learn in her life?

"How did you know this poem?" I asked "Is it written down in some book?"

"No, the young one who wrote it was my great, great grandmother." Pausing for a moment, he continued "I suppose she was happy. But then, we are all as happy as we want to be."

His message "we are all as happy as we want to be" continues to resonate with me. How often have we sought contentment and fulfillment by looking in the wrong places? The reality is that the happiest people seem to be those who work to give happiness to others. Everyone prefers the company of givers. Takers deplete energy. Givers create an environment where people can be themselves. It is the givers that connect with the magic. The remarkable Australian psychiatrist W. Beran Wolfe, in his famous text "How to Be Happy Though Human" made it clear; the ingredients of happiness are simple. Happiness cannot be bought; indeed, money has very little to do with it. He felt people are unhappy because they look inward instead of outward. They worry too much about what they lack, about circumstances they cannot change, about things they feel they must have or must be before they can lead full and satisfying lives. He came to the conclusion that:

> "If you observe a really happy man you will find him building a boat, writing a symphony, educating his son, growing double dahlias in his garden. He will not be searching for happiness as if it were a gold collar button that has rolled under the cupboard in his bedroom. He will have become aware that he is happy in the course of living 24 crowded hours of the day.
>
> If you live only for yourself you are always in immediate danger of being bored to death with the repetition of your own views and interests. No one has learned the meaning of living until he has surrendered his ego to the service of his fellowmen. For those who seek the larger happiness and greater effectiveness open to human beings there can be but one philosophy of life, a philosophy of constructive altruism. "

The more we give to life, the more we get back. It is a universal law, and it is one of the most powerful factors in being happy on this planet.

Chapter Fifteen

The most important things in life are the ones done with love

"There are two ways of spreading light: to be the candle or the mirror that reflects it."

Edith Wharton

"One word frees us of all the weight and pain of life. That word is love." Written over 2,400 years ago by Sophocles

I think of airports when I get down about the world. It is where boyfriends and girlfriends squeeze each other, where soldiers returning from duty hug their crying mothers. It is where husbands and wives walk hand in hand smiling with contentment and grandparents bend over to catch grandchildren as they race towards them yelling "Grandpa! Grandma!" It is where old friends greet each other with bear hugs. It is where you hear "I love you" and "I missed you." Love really is all around.

When we start to look for the better part of ourselves we always come back to love. I have learned that to love abundantly is to live abundantly. "You will find as you look back upon your life, that the moments that stand out, the moments when you have really lived, are the moments when you have done things in a spirit of love." So wrote Henry Drummond, the famous Scottish evangelical writer, in his famous essay on love.

Why then do so many of us have difficulty connecting with love and even come to feel unloving towards ourselves and others at times? Essentially we have fallen out of love. Judgment, condemnation, and criticism of ourselves and others wall us off. It is part of the original Fall. As fragmented creatures, our job is to reconnect to each other just as Jesus came to show us over two thousand years ago. As Emerson put it "Love is our highest word and the synonym for God." The more we grow in love, through thought and deed, the greater inner joy we experience and more forgiving we become. Feelings of fear, doubt, and unworthiness weaken as they cannot exist with love, and our lives become guided by higher principles and not ruled by events and the need for other's approval. As we grow to be vessels filled with God's love we become a healing and illuminating influence on others. Our cup overflows. Joy and miracles follow. Emmet Fox said, "If only you could love enough you would be the happiest and most powerful being in the world."

Love is that inner quality that sees good everywhere and in everybody. It makes no notice of faults. It is the great harmonizer in life, and once the spark is kindled within, it can't help but flow to others.

In one of her first duties as a young minister, my sister Cathy was asked to visit someone at a hospital. Her youthful looks didn't help dressed in a suit and little bow tie. She went up to the nurses' station and asked to see this one particular patient.

They asked "Are you family?" "No. I am a minister." They snickered. Cathy rolled her eyes and as she approached the door to the hospital room, she saw a sign that gloves and a mask were required to enter. Inside was a skinny girl about 13 years old with scabs all over her body. Cathy realized this unfortunate soul had the dreaded AIDS virus. Back in the early 1980s AIDS was something to be feared and her first inclination was to walk out. Cathy told her who she was. The girl explained that she no longer received visits from her family. They were afraid to see her. That everyone was afraid of her. She said her fear was "To die alone."

Cathy excused herself for a moment and went out to the hallway and began to cry. "God", she said, "I don't know how to do this. I don't know what to do. Help me." The message she got was clear. This is a child of God, not someone to be feared. Look through the eyes of God and love her.

Cathy went back in the room, talked some more and then climbed onto the bed, put the child's head on her shoulder, and reassured her "You are not going to die alone…I will be here with you." So each day Cathy visited her. On some days holding her hand; other days holding her in her arms. On her final day, Cathy crawled onto the bed and just held her. She loved her. She held her until the child took her last breath and passed away.

What I have learned in life is that those who give their life to love have nothing to lose and only grow richer. My sister is one of the wealthiest people I know.

Chapter Sixteen

There is a natural rhythm to the universe

"Live each season as it passes; breathe the air, drink the drink, taste the fruit, and resign yourself to the influences of each."

Henry David Thoreau

Theoretical physicists and mystical shamans are arriving at a mutual understanding: the universe is alive. We do not need billion dollar atom smashers or to spend years meditating to witness the divine flowing through all of life. Simply look up at night to the stars. There is a natural rhythm to life.

Nothing stands still in this universe. Tides sweep in. Tides sweep out. The sun rises. The sun sets. There is birth. There is death. Every beginning has an ending; all endings herald a new beginning. Throughout this ebb and flow there is the realization that time is precious. There is also the realization that it all is borrowed. For some of us the days are shorter. But there is enough beauty in the hours we have, if we only stop to appreciate it. If we but stop to treasure the friendships, the laughter with friends, the love we have for each other. If we but stop to help someone we don't know and connect with the majesty of life. Above all, if we use the time we have to learn, grow, and expand in this magnificent world, "The whole life of the individual is nothing but the process of giving birth to himself," according to Eric Fromm.

A good life is a life where one has learned. A Hindu proverb put it this way, "There is nothing noble in being superior to some other man. The true nobility is in being superior to your previous self." If we can leave this world smarter, wiser, with a larger capacity to give kindness and love, then it is a good life. We grow to heaven, we don't go to heaven.

Life is a voyage that's homeward bound. It is a natural transition keeping with the ebb and flow of the universe. As long as we understand that each moment has a life unto itself with as much possibility for joy and happiness as we are able to bring to it, then death is only a passage to what Kahlil Gibran calls "the distant shore" where even more beautiful moments await us. We are all on a journey - a journey towards inheritance. Like the prodigal son, our journey takes us back to a God who smiles, a God who plays, a God who laughs, a God who cries, and most importantly a God who loves us unconditionally. For this I am grateful beyond words.

As ALS impairs my body's ability to function, I am becoming something new. Part of me transitions to that "distant shore" each night. My soul comes back larger as my body becomes smaller. The mornings always arrive too swiftly, and as I wake up to a world of phone calls and daily activity, there is recognition that this activity, this life, this maya, is simply an experience in the middle of eternity. And that we, as forever beings, take the experiences and lessons learned during this physical dance when we leave here, and nothing else. As the old time preacher said: "Hearses do not have luggage racks."

Over two thousand years ago, the stoic Roman emperor and philosopher, Marcus Aurelius commented: "…serenely greet the journey's end as an olive falls when it is ripe, blessing the branch that bares it, and giving thanks to the tree that gave it life." This is the best way to face death - with gratitude; with gratitude for the love that has enlarged me; with gratitude for the opportunities to help others; with gratitude for the problems that made me grow; with gratitude for the support, seen and unseen, from our loving creator along the way.

Thomas Sugrue, author of *There is a River*, put it this way:

The Great Mind is the Mind of God to which your mind must return. And the Great Heart is the Heart of God, to which your heart must return. Then your thoughts will share the thoughts of all creation and your heart will beat with the heart of God.

But now you are alone. You were sent on a long adventure to help God bring creation to flower. You are his agent, bearing his love. Your heart is faintly echoing His song. Make yourself a part of that song, that those who have lost the tune may remember it again, through you. Consider not whether you are fed, or clothed or housed, but only whether you love, and pray, and serve. When you rest, let Him hold you. When you reach out, touch his hand and then put your arm around a friend.

There is much to be thankful for on this road called life.

The Grateful Road

On this road you will find that we are all together.

Some of us walk faster.

Some of us carry others.

Some of us actually go back to help those who are stuck.

We all take side trips down meandering paths, richer
    and wiser for the experience.

Somewhere during this journey you will become aware
    that all is love.

False gods of fear, anger, resentment, and self-centeredness
    disappear.

It is then that you become a beacon for others, able to
    forgive, laugh, and love, regardless of circumstance.

It is then that you will have arrived back home.

Chris H. Norman

To experience the *What I Have Learned* slide presentation set to music, please go to:

http://www.whatihavelearned.org

Please send any comments or uplifting stories to whatihavelearned@msn.com

About the Author

Chris Norman's passion has luckily been his career. He helps consumer brand companies become more effective at retail through displays and product packaging. It is an intriguing world of consumer behavior, where color, shape, and message can make the difference between success and failure of products in the ever competitive marketplace.

Diagnosed with Amyotrophic Lateral Sclerosis (ALS), also known as Lou Gehrig's disease, the day before his fiftieth birthday, Chris has been blessed with the support and love of strong family and friends. He lives with his wife, son and daughter, and three dogs (Bubba, Louie, and Sky) in Richmond, Virginia.

The book, *The Grateful Road*, is an effort to impart the key learnings he has had in life to his two children.

<u>About Amyotrophic Lateral Sclerosis (ALS), or Lou Gehrig's Disease</u>

ALS is a rare and fatal neuromuscular disease that strikes 3,000 to 5,000 people in the United States each year. Very little is known about the disease. It is a debilitating disease that affects the ability of motor neurons to function. As of this writing, there is no cure.

CPSIA information can be obtained
at www.ICGtesting.com
Printed in the USA
FSOW02n0141121216
28458FS